MOTIVATION LOMBARDI STYLE

A collection of thoughts from the
legendary coach about the athletic playing field
and the business battlefield

Graphics by Balance Design

LOMBARDI

Lombardi

Vince Lombardi believed that the ingredients of greatness are not necessarily inherent traits, but rather qualities to be encouraged and cultivated. He felt that no matter what the endeavor, one's desire, not ability, determines success. Through his "total dedication" to the heights of human potential, football's legendary coach created champions.

Discipline, intensity and sacrifice were among the convictions that dominated his own life and that of anyone with the talent and tenacity to play for him. Both admired and feared, Lombardi could arouse strong emotions and elicit decisive results. Using keen insights, clever anecdotes and unyielding intimidation when necessary, he forced those around him to exceed their physical and mental limitations.

The meaning and importance of Lombardi's lessons transcend sports. As the thoughts documented in this book clearly demonstrate, Vince Lombardi recognized the many correlations between the game of football and the game of life; the athletic playing field and the business battlefield.

Intensity

"There's only one way to succeed in anything, and that is to give it everything. I do, and I demand that my players do."

"If you aren't fired with enthusiasm, you'll be fired with enthusiasm."

INTENSITY

Success

"Success demands singleness of purpose."

"Mental toughness is essential to success."

"You never win a game unless you beat the guy in front of you. The score on the board doesn't mean a thing. That's for the fans. You've got to win the war with the man in front of you. You've got to get your man."

Sacrifice

"To achieve success, whatever the job we have, we must pay a price."

"Success is like anything worthwhile. It has a price. You have to pay the price to win and you have to pay the price to get to the point where success is possible. Most important, you must pay the price to stay there."

"Football is a great deal like life in that it teaches that work, sacrifice, perseverance, competitive drive, selflessness and respect for authority is the price that each and every one of us must pay to achieve any goal that is worthwhile."

BELIEF

Belief

"Confidence is contagious and so is lack of confidence, and a customer will recognize both."

"If you believe in yourself and have the courage, the determination, the dedication, the competitive drive and if you are willing to sacrifice the little things in life and pay the price for the things that are worthwhile, it can be done."

"Unless a man believes in himself and makes a total commitment to his career and puts everything he has into it – his mind, his body and his heart – what is life worth to him? If I were a salesman, I would make this commitment to my company, to the product and most of all, to myself."

"The quality of a person's life is in direct proportion to their commitment to excellence, regardless of their chosen field of endeavor."

"Once a man has made a commitment to a way of life, he puts the greatest strength in the world behind him. It's something we call heart power. Once a man has made this commitment, nothing will stop him short of success."

"It's not whether you get knocked down, it's whether you get up."

COMMITMENT

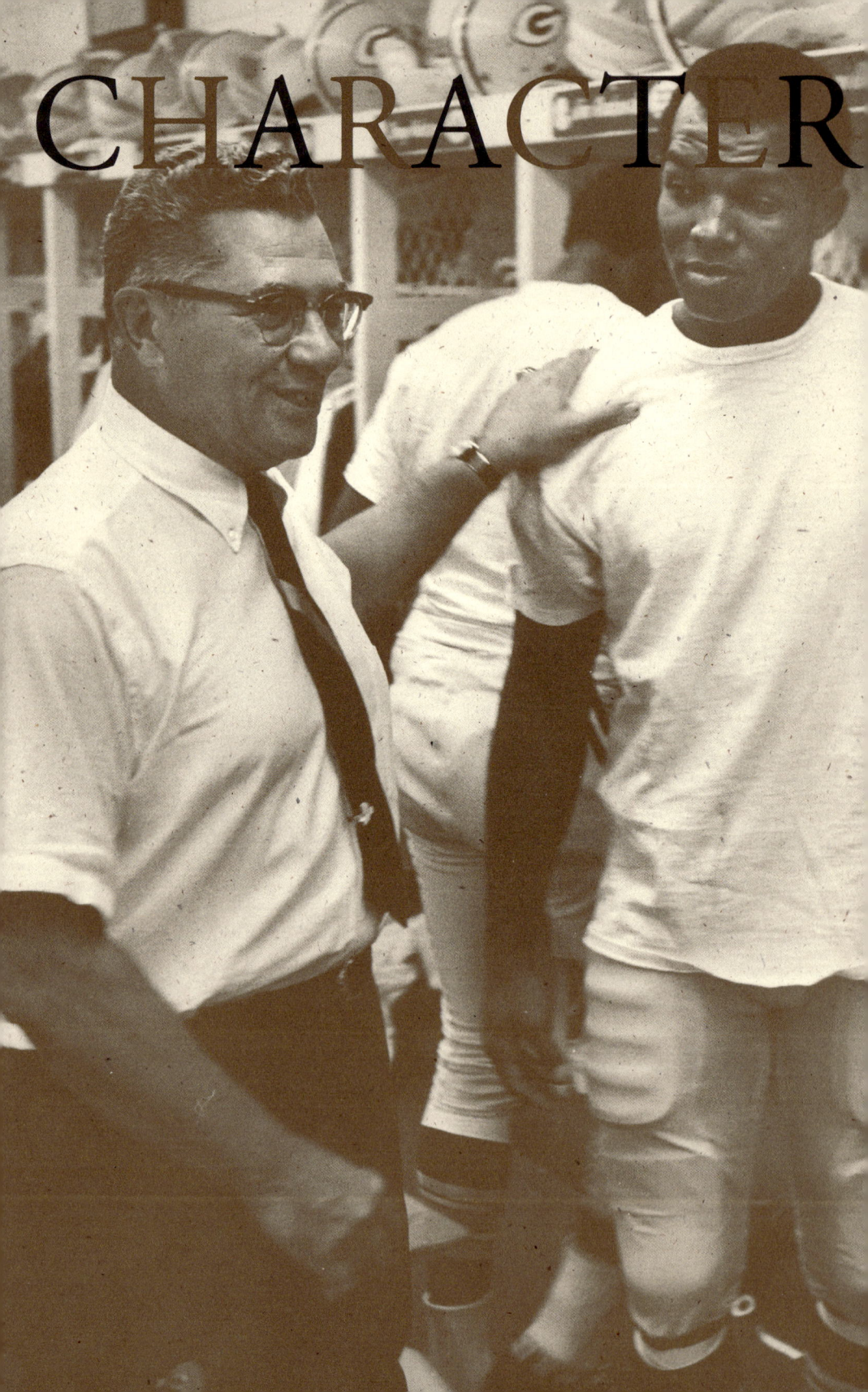

CHARACTER

Character

"It is essential to understand that battles are primarily won in the hearts of men."

"In great attempts, it is glorious even to fail."

"They may not love you at the time, but they will later."

Leadership

"Leadership rests not only upon ability, not only upon capacity; having the capacity to lead is not enough. The leader must be willing to use it. His leadership is then based on truth and character. There must be truth in the purpose and will power in the character."

LEADERSHIP

LEADERSHIP

Leadership

"Leadership is based on a spiritual quality; the power to inspire, the power to inspire others to follow."

"Having the capacity to lead is not enough. The leader must be willing to use it."

"Leaders are made, they are not born. They are made by hard effort, which is the price which all of us must pay to achieve any goal that is worthwhile."

"A leader must identify himself with the group, must back up the group, even at the risk of displeasing superiors. He must believe that the group wants from him a sense of approval. If this feeling prevails, production, discipline, morale will be high, and in return, you can demand the cooperation to promote the goals of the company."

"The harder you work, the harder it is to surrender."

"They call it coaching but it is teaching. You do not just tell them... you show them the reasons."

"Once you have established the goals you want and the price you're willing to pay, you can ignore the minor hurts, the opponent's pressure and the temporary failures."

PREPARATION

DESIRE

Desire

"The difference between a successful person and others is not a lack of strength, not a lack of knowledge, but rather in a lack of will."

"The spirit, the will to win and the will to excel - these are the things that endure and these are the qualities that are so much more important than any of the events that occasion them."

"It is essential to understand that battles are primarily won in the hearts of men. Men respond to leadership in a most remarkable way and once you have won his heart, he will follow you anywhere."

Discipline

"I've never known a man worth his salt who in the long run, deep down in his heart, didn't appreciate the grind, the discipline. There is something good in men that really yearns for discipline."

DISCIPLINE

Discipline

"The good Lord gave you a body that can stand most anything. It's your mind you have to convince.

"Mental toughness is many things and rather difficult to explain. Its qualities are sacrifice and self-denial. Also, most importantly, it is combined with a perfectly disciplined will that refuses to give in. It's a state of mind – you could call it character in action."

Teamwork

"Individual commitment to a group effort - that is what makes a team work, a company work, a society work, a civilization work."

"Teams do not go physically flat, they go mentally stale."

"A leader must believe in teamwork through participation. He can never close the gap between himself and the group. He must walk, as it were, a tightrope between the consent he must win and the control he must exert."

TEAMWORK

WINNING

Winning

"I firmly believe that any man's finest hour - his greatest fulfillment to all he holds dear - is that moment when he has worked his heart out in a good cause and lies exhausted on the field of battle - victorious."

Winning

"Winning is not everything – but making the effort to win is."

"Some of us will do our jobs well and some will not, but we will all be judged by only one thing – the result."

"Winning is not a sometime thing: it's an all the time thing. You don't win once in a while; you don't do the right thing once in a while; you do them right all the time. Winning is a habit. Unfortunately, so is losing."

WINNING

WHAT IT TAKES TO BE NUMBER ONE

Lombardi

Winning is not a sometime thing; it's an all the time thing. You don't win once in a while; you don't do things right once in a while; you do them right all the time. Winning is a habit. Unfortunately, so is losing.

There is no room for second place. There is only one place in my game, and that's first place. I have finished second twice in my time at Green Bay, and I don't ever want to finish second again. There is a second place bowl game, but it is a game for losers played by losers. It is and always has been an American zeal to be first in anything we do, and to win, and to win, and to win.

Lombardi

Every time a football player goes to ply his trade he's got to play from the ground up – from the soles of his feet right up to his head. Every inch of him has to play. Some guys play with their heads. That's O.K. You've got to be smart to be number one in any business. But more importantly, you've got to play with your heart, with every fiber of your body. If you're lucky enough to find a guy with a lot of head and a lot of heart, he's never going to come off the field second.

Running a football team is no different than running any other kind of organization – an army, a political party or a business. The principles are the same. The object is to win – to beat the other guy. Maybe that sounds hard or cruel. I don't think it is.

It is a reality of life that men are competitive and the most competitive games draw the most competitive men. That's why they are there – to compete. To know the rules and objectives when they get in the game. The object is to win fairly, squarely, by the rules – but to win.

Lombardi

And in truth, I've never known a man worth his salt who in the long run, deep down in his heart, didn't appreciate the grind, the discipline. There is something in good men that really yearns for discipline and the harsh reality of head to head combat.

I don't say these things because I believe in the "brute" nature of man or that men must be brutalized to be combative. I believe in God, and I believe in human decency. But I firmly believe that any man's finest hour – his greatest fulfillment to all he holds dear – is that moment when he has to work his heart out in a good cause and he's exhausted on the field of battle – victorious.

Vince Lombardi

Lombardi

"When Lombardi said 'sit down' we didn't look for a chair." *Forrest Gregg*

"It was a helluva performance to listen to when he'd go out there and get his troops around him. He laughed. He cried. He prayed. He motivated. I think he could motivate almost anybody to do almost anything. He communicated with human emotions." *Chuck Lane*

"He made us realize that if the mind was willing, the body can go." *Forrest Gregg*

"He made you a believer. He told you what the other team was going to do, and he told you what you had to do to beat them, and invariably he was right." *Willie Davis*

"He made us all better than we thought we could be."
Jerry Kramer

Lombardi

"He pushed you to the end of your endurance and then beyond it. And if there was reserve there, well he found that too." *Henry Jordan*

"No matter how mad he got, he never stopped thinking. That's something. His mind always was going. And it seemed like the more angry he got the harder his mind worked. Maybe anger made his mind better." *Mark Duncan*

"All he wanted from you was perfection." *Jim Taylor*

"Coach Lombardi showed me that by working hard and using my mind, I could overcome my weakness to the point where I could be one of the best." *Bart Starr*

Lombardi

"He prepared us so well, and he motivated us so well, I felt he was a part of me on the field." *Fuzzy Thurston*

"His enthusiasm, his spirit, was infectious." *Frank Gifford*

"You had to stand up and do what was demanded of you. If it was windy, he wouldn't accept the wind as an excuse or if the ground were frozen you weren't allowed to slip. You had to adjust. He never said, 'That would have been a good pass except the wind was bad.' Never." *Zeke Bratkowski*

"He told us we were going to be a team. We were going to rise and fall on our faces together." *Sonny Jurgensen*

"Respect wasn't a one way street with him. He demanded it of others but he also gave it." *Pete Rozelle*

"He was a master at handling and inspiring us. He's the kind of man you just had to win for." *Paul Hornung*

Lombardi

"The fear in my mind was not him but that for some reason I would not be a part of this team and be with this man." *Forrest Gregg*

"He had a hard exterior but he also had a big, soft heart." *Ray Nitschke*

"He was very much interested in the total man as far as his players were concerned. I know that he was very interested in the fact that guys be total citizens. In other words, that we not only be good football players and winners, but that we be the type of people, citizens the town would be proud of." *Carroll Dale*

"He didn't push; he led." *Henry Jordan*

"He was an innovator, willing to experiment to make his team more effective." *Merv Hyman*

Lombardi

"You might reduce Lombardi's coaching philosophy to a single sentence: In any game, you do the things you do best and you do them over and over and over." *George Halas*

"I loved him because of his total absence of hypocrisy. I loved him because he was the best there ever was at what he did. I loved him because he had the curious capacity for making young men responsive to him without their feeling they had been abused." *Howard Cosell*

The cost is low...
but the ideas are priceless!

Each title in the Successories "Power of One" library takes less than 30 minutes to read, but the wisdom it contains will last a lifetime. Take advantage of volume pricing as you share these insights with all the people who impact your career, your business, your life.

Anatomy of A Leader
This collection of insights written by Carl Mays represents a simple thought-provoking body of knowledge that can help everyone develop the qualities of a leader. #713259

Attitude: Your Internal Compass
Denis Waitley and Boyd Matheson give powerful examples of how a slight shift in the way you see the world can yield powerful results in an ever-changing workplace. #713193

Burn Brightly Without Burning Out
This book, by motivational expert Dick Biggs, will boost morale and productivity by helping people balance the work they do with the life they lead. #716016

Companies Don't Succeed...People Do
Successories founder and Chairman, Mac Anderson, outlines "The Art of Recognition" – how to develop employees and a recognition culture within any organization. #716015

Dare to Soar
The spirit of eagles inspired this unique collection of motivational thoughts by noted speaker Byrd Baggett. Any goal can be reached if you "Dare to Soar." #716006

The Employee Connection
Noted employee motivation expert Jim Harris provides dozens of practical methods for leaders to "unleash the power of their people." #716018

Empowerment
Ken Blanchard and Susan Fowler Woodring's valuable insights into empowerment outlines how to achieve "Peak Performance Through Self-Leadership." #716022

Motivating Today's Employees
Recognition expert Bob Nelson offers a great primer on the impact of employee rewards and recognition. #716007

Motivating Yourself
Mac Anderson, Successories founder and Chairman, offers a mix of proven ideas and motivational thoughts to help "Recharge the Human Battery." #716021

Motivation, Lombardi Style
Use the coach's memorable collection of insights about the athletic playing field and the business battlefield to inspire your team. #716013

Pulling Together
Nationally-noted author and speaker, John Murphy, outlines "17 Principles for Effective Teamwork" with a refreshing mix of information and thought-provoking questions. #716019

Quality, Service, Teamwork
Share these "Foundations of Excellence" with your employees! This valuable resource includes over 100 motivational quotes. #716014

Results
Help your sales team turn passion into profit and maximize their relationship power with these proven strategies for changing times. Jeff Blackman's experience and style makes this an entertaining handbook that guarantees results. #716017

Rule #One
Author and customer service expert C. Leslie Charles has compiled dozens of insightful ideas, common sense tips and easy-to-apply rules in this customer service handbook. #716008

Teamwork
Noted consultant Glenn Parker gives managers, team leaders and members a valuable blueprint for successful team building. Put it to work for your team! #716012

Think Change
This intriguing book, by John Murphy, challenges today's employees to change their thinking to keep up with an evolving workplace. "Adapt and Thrive or Fall Behind." #716020

To order call toll-free 800-535-2773